Guinea Pig

Acknowledgements

The Publisher would like to thank the following for photographic contributions:
Cover image (main) © istockphoto.com/Eline Spek
Cover images (insets) © Southern Cavy Club; istockphoto.com/Jaimie D Travis;
istockphoto.com/Ralph Loesche; istockphoto.com/Eline Spek
Endpapers © istockphoto.com/Ralph Loesche
Page 1 © istockphoto.com/Eline Spek
Page 4, Oxford Scientific, Aland and Sandy Carey;
Page 6, Oxford Scientific, Paul Franklin;
Pages 12-15 © Southern Cavy Club
Page 18 © Rosie Ray
Page 19, Tony Northrup, www.northrup.org;
Page 22 © istockphoto.com/Jaimie D Travis
Page 26 © Southern Cavy Club
Page 27 © Rosie Ray
Page 29 © istockphoto.com/Eline Spek
Page 30 © Rosie Ray

© The Pet Book Publishing Company 2007

ALL RIGHTS RESERVED

Contents

Looking Back

The ancestors of our pet guinea pigs lived in Peru, in South America.

Guinea pigs are members of the rodent family, which is the largest group of mammals on earth. Rodents look very different from each other, but they all share one feature. They have four big front teeth, which they use for gnawing. The family name 'rodent' comes from the Latin name 'rodere', which means to gnaw. The front teeth, (known as incisors) grow throughout a guinea pig's life.

The hunted

The wild ancestor of the guinea pig is known as the *Cavia cutleri*, which means the Restless Cavy. It is still found in South America. The guinea pig

The wild cavy lives on open grasslands and has to be on the alert.

Like their wild ancestors, guinea pigs produce young that are very advanced at birth. These piglets are only 10 days old.

is also known as the cavy, which is the name that breeders and other experts prefer to use.

In the wild, cavies graze on grass and plants and are on constant lookout for meat-eating predators. They are in danger of being hunted by bigger animals and by birds of prey. Living in constant danger makes wild cavies alert, fast-moving, and nervous, and you can see this behaviour in pet guinea pigs today.

Family life

Wild cavies sometimes make use of burrows left by other animals, but mostly they live in the open. There are usually between five and ten cavies in a group. There is a male (boar),

several females (sows), and their young, known as piglets.

As cavies give birth in the open, their young have to be ready to look after themselves almost from day one. For this reason, piglets are very advanced at birth:

- They are born with their eyes open.
- They have a full coat.
- They have teeth already cut.
- Within a few days, the piglets can eat solid food.

Cavy Care

In order to produce young that are so well developed, female cavies have a long pregnancy, lasting between 59 and 72 days.

The Human Link

The cavies of South America were brought in from the wild and used as food.

The Incas of Peru first caught guinea pigs from the wild around 5000 BC. These little animals were used for food, but were kept rather like pets. Guinea pigs were allowed to run around the floors of the Incas' homes, and were fed with scraps from the table.

On special occasions, guinea pigs were sacrificed as part of a religious ceremony, and then eaten.

To be sure of a constant supply of guinea pigs, the Incas kept the animals in enclosed areas and allowed them to breed.

Guinea pigs are sociable animals and are happy to be kept in large groups.

Guinea pigs soon became popular as pets.

Spanish conquest

The Spanish invaded Peru in the 15th Century, and they took an interest in the guinea pigs kept by the Incas. When the Spanish soldiers returned to Europe, they took guinea pigs to eat on the journey. The guinea pigs that were not eaten were taken home as pets. The Spanish people were delighted with the charming little animals from South America, and from then on, guinea pigs were kept as pets in both Spain and Portugal.

News of guinea pigs spread, and soon they were being kept in other European countries, including England.

In those days, guinea pigs were expensive to buy, and so only rich families could keep them as pets.

What's in a name?

When the guinea pig was prepared for the table it looked like a little pig, and the Spanish gave it the name 'Cochinillo' which means "little pig". It is not certain where the 'guinea' part of its name comes from. It could be that when guinea pigs first arrived in Europe as pets they were sold for a guinea (about £1.05), which was a lot of money in those days.

Did You Know?

Guinea pigs in South America are still used as a source of food. In Peru, Bolivia and Ecuador, roasted guinea pig is a popular dish.

Perfect Pets

Guinea pigs are among the most popular of the small animals that are kept as pets.

There are many reasons why the guinea pig is a great pet to keep:

- Guinea pigs are gentle creatures that rarely bite or scratch.
- Guinea pigs are larger than many of the small animal pets, such as hamsters and gerbils, so they are easier to handle.
- They are active throughout the day (some small animals, such as hamsters, are more lively at night).
- They can live in an outdoor hutch, or be kept in the house in a cage.
- There are lots of colours and coat types to choose from.
- If they are looked after properly, they have few health problems.

In time, you can build up a close relationship with your guinea pig.

- Guinea pigs live for around six years, which is longer than other small animal pets.
- If you have an allergy to pets with fur, you can still choose a guinea pig if it can live in an outside hutch.

Special needs

Do not be tempted to rush out and buy a guinea pig because you think it will be easy to look after. Like all living creatures, guinea pigs have their own special needs:

- A guinea pig will be unhappy on its own, so plan to keep more than one.
- Guinea pigs need secure, comfortable housing, with

enough room to move about.
- The hutch or cage needs to be kept clean.
- Long-haired guinea pigs must be groomed, and teeth and nails must be checked so they do not grow too long.
- You will need to arrange care for your guinea pigs when you are on holiday.

A guinea pig is an inquisitive animal and is interested in everything that is going on.

The Guinea Pig

Find out how its body works and how it sees the world.

Eyes

A guinea pig can see in front and to the side without moving its head, which helps it to spot predators in the wild. A guinea pig can pick up sudden movements and can see primary colours (red, blue and green), but their sight is not as good as ours.

Nose

The guinea pig has a good sense of smell, which it uses to recognise other guinea pigs. A guinea pig will also get to know the smell of its owner. Guinea pigs choose food by smell, and keep away from poisonous plants.

Teeth

A guinea pig's teeth grow all the time. In total, it has 20 teeth; the four incisors (the front teeth that are used for biting) are just behind the lips.

Front feet

Each front foot has four claws.

Ears

The ears are hairless. Depending on the variety of guinea pig, the ears can be small and upright, large and rose-shaped, or drooping. A guinea pig's sense of hearing is twice as powerful as ours.

Whiskers

These are very sensitive, and a guinea pig uses them to find its way in the dark. A guinea pig will use its whiskers to work out if it can fit into a space.

Coat

This can be short, long or rough-haired. The coat may be all one colour, a mixture of colours, or with special markings.

Body

The body is short and compact.

Back feet

Each back foot has three claws.

Tail

You cannot see a tail because it is so short that it does not come outside the body. There are eight tailbones that can be felt under the skin.

Cavy varieties

Guinea pigs have different types of coat, and there is a fantastic range of colours and markings to choose from.

Guinea pigs are popular as pets, but there are also a large number of enthusiasts who breed and show purebred cavies.

Starting with a small, brown-coloured guinea pig from South America, breeders have developed new breeds that look very different from their wild ancestors.

You may not want to show guinea pigs, but it is interesting to look at the different breeds that are available.

Coat types

Guinea pigs come in four major coat types:

- **Smooth:** These are the short-haired guinea pigs. This coat type is also known as English, American or Bolivian.
- **Abyssinian:** These are rough-coated guinea pigs. The coat does not grow straight, but is arranged in ridges and swirls, which are known as rosettes.

This guinea pig, which is a self lilac, has a short, smooth coat that is easy to look after.

This brindle-coloured guinea pig has a rough coat, typical of an Abyssinian.

- **Long:** Long-haired guinea pigs, such as the Peruvian and the Sheltie (or Silkie), have amazingly long coats. Sometimes you can hardly see the shape of the guinea pig underneath all the hair!
- **Rex:** This variety has a woolly coat that stands upright.

Cavy Care

There are many crossbreed guinea pigs, which come in lots of colours and coat types. You cannot exhibit a crossbreed in the show ring, but they make excellent pets.

This guinea pig is long-haired. Guinea pig hair is more like human hair than like rabbit fur, and needs regular brushing and combing. This is the Sheltie variety.

There are some other interesting coat types. The crested guinea pig has a crest of hair that grows on the top of its head, which may be a different colour from the rest of its coat, or the same colour. The satin guinea pig has a fine, silky coat which has a beautiful shine to it.

Colours

Breeders have developed a wide range of colours, markings, and colour combinations.

Self-coloured

These guinea pigs are one colour all over, and they are all smooth-haired. They are known as self-coloured. The colours include:

• White
• Cream
• Golden
• Black
• Chocolate
• Red (a rich mahogany shade)
• Beige
• Lilac (a shade of light grey).

Some of these varieties also have special eye colours, and may be either red-eyed or black-eyed.

Marked

These are the guinea pigs with more than one colour in their

Self-coloured: This guinea pig has a chocolate coloured coat.

Himalayan: A beautifully marked guinea pig.

coats. They are known as 'marked'. Colour combinations and markings include:

- **Dutch:** A coloured guinea pig with white face markings and a white saddle.
- **Agouti:** There are two shades on each hair, creating a banded effect. There are a number of agouti colours, such as silver agouti, golden agouti and cinnamon agouti.
- **Tortoiseshell and white:** This is a mix of red, black and white.

- **Himalayan:** This guinea pig has a white body with dark hair around the nose and ears.
- **Dalmatian:** This is a spotted variety, with the same markings as a Dalmatian dog.

Breeders like inventing new colours. Some of the more exotic colours include buff, which is a dark cream, and sable, where the guinea pig has chocolate-coloured hair on its back that becomes a lighter cream colour on its sides and belly.

The Peruvian: The hair on top of the body lies towards the head and falls over the face – so you can't tell which end is which.

Setting Up Home

Living quarters need to be safe, secure and comfortable.

Guinea pigs will live happily in an outdoor hutch. In the coldest winter months, you will need to move the hutch somewhere warmer, such as a draught-free shed. When you choose a hutch, look for the following features:

- Buy the biggest hutch you can afford so that your guinea pigs have plenty of space to move around.
- The hutch should be raised off the ground at least 23 cm to protect the guinea pigs from draughts, as well as from enemies such as cats and foxes.
- The guinea pig will need a sleeping compartment sectioned off from the main part of the hutch.
- The wire netting covering the front area of the hutch must be narrow enough to stop mice and rats getting in.
- The hutch fastenings must be secure.

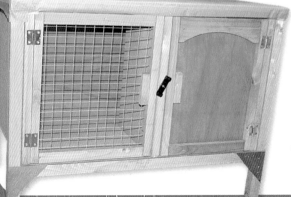

The hutch should be positioned in a sheltered place, which is free from draughts.

Cavy Care

Do not move your guinea pigs' hutch to a garage in the cold weather, as the fumes from a car could kill the animals.

Indoor home

Guinea pigs can be kept as house pets. You will need a cage that is big enough for your guinea pigs to run around freely. You will also need a larger exercise area, outside the cage, which is safe and secure.

If you are planning to keep guinea pigs indoors, consider these points:

• Guinea pigs do not like loud noises. They will prefer to be kept in a quiet room, such as the utility room, rather than the main living room.

• Guinea pigs should be kept at room temperature, which is around 18-22 degrees Centigrade.

Bedding

The best type of bedding to use is wood shavings. You can top this up with a layer of hay in the sleeping area, so that your guinea pigs are snug and warm.

Water

Your guinea pig must have fresh water available at all times. It is best to use a water bottle, which can be attached to the side of the hutch or cage.

Indoor homes are made especially for guinea pigs.

It's Playtime!

Guinea pigs are lively, active animals that love to climb and explore.

Cavy Care

Make sure your guinea pigs have at least one session a day in their exercise area, lasting around an hour.

Guinea pigs enjoy spending time in an outside run.

Guinea pigs enjoy time outside their hutch, when they can be free to graze and to run around. Most runs for small animals are triangular in shape, and measure about 3m in length and 90cm in height. There should be a covered area where the guinea pigs can find shelter.

Guinea pigs love to sunbathe, but care is needed as they can overdo it! They have no hair on their ears, and these can get sunburnt. Make sure the run is positioned so part of it is in the shade. Remember to move the run to a new patch every

You can buy an activity ball, so when your guinea pig pushes it along, treats drop out.

day so that there is fresh grass to graze. Don't forget to attach a water bottle to the run, and keep it topped up.

Indoor Play Pen

If you are keeping your guinea pigs in the house, they will need time outside their cage in an exercise area. You can let your guinea pigs go free if you have a safe room, but it is safer to use a playpen. You can buy an exercise pen for small animals, or you can adapt a child's play pen.

- The ideal size for two or three guinea pigs is 1 metre by 1.25 m.
- The playpen must be escape-proof.
- You will need a shallow plastic tray to cover the base of the playpen, which you can fill with wood shavings.

Toys

Guinea pigs do not play with toys as much as small pets such as hamsters and gerbils because they cannot 'hold' toys with their front feet. But guinea pigs love to gnaw. They will enjoy 'chew' toys. The best type are hard wooden toys made for parrots.

Hiding places, such as tunnels and cardboard boxes with holes cut out, are also a favourite.

Guinea pigs love to explore hidey-holes.

The Right Choice

Signs of a healthy guinea pig.

Look for a guinea pig that is active, alert,
and interested in its surroundings.

Coat
This should be
glossy and clean,
with no bald
patches.

Skin
There should be
no sign of
soreness, or
flaky skin.

Ears
Check the
ears are
clean.

Eyes
Look for
bright and
clear eyes.

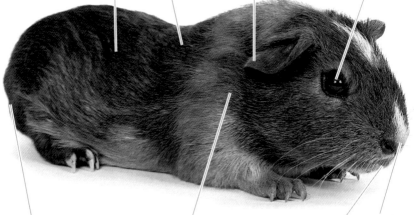

Anus
If hair around the
anus is matted, it
could mean the
guinea pig is suffering
from diarrhoea.

Body
The guinea pig's
body should be
plump, with no
bumps or
swellings.

Mouth
There should
be no
dribbling
from the
mouth.

Nostrils
The
nostrils
should be
free from
discharge.

There is a wide variety of guinea pigs to choose from. At Pets At Home stores the guinea pigs are kept in spacious runs so you have a good opportunity to watch them and make your choice.

Male or female?

The staff at Pets At Home will be able to tell you which are boars, and which are sows. The male will grow slightly bigger than the female. Males like attention from people, and are often more ready to play. Females take longer to settle, but they also make wonderful pets.

If you do not plan to breed guinea pigs, buy either two males or two females. If you buy both animals as youngsters they will grow up together and will become close friends.

Guinea pigs enjoy company, and you will often see them close together, or even feeding from the same bowl.

Making Friends

Guinea pigs are timid animals, and will be worried about settling in a new home.

Y ou will be longing to play with your guinea pigs, but try to be patient. The guinea pigs need to explore their new home, and to get used to their new surroundings. You should put food in the hutch or cage, but the guinea pigs may not be ready to eat straight away.

Handling

When your guinea pigs seem relaxed and happy in their new surroundings, you can start to handle them. If you handle them gently, they will become tame and will enjoy being stroked and cuddled in your lap.

The correct way to hold a guinea pig is to get a firm grasp around its shoulders, and support its weight with your other hand, under its rear end.

It may take some time, but if are gentle and patient, your guinea pig will learn to trust you.

A guinea pig will not struggle if you hold it the correct way.

The safest way to handle your guinea pig is when you are sitting on the floor. Guinea pigs move very quickly, and it is all too easy for accidents to happen.

Giving treats

The way to a guinea pig's heart is via its stomach! Guinea pigs love tasty treats, such as a slice of carrot or apple. Tempt your guinea pig with its favourite food and it will soon be eating from your fingers. Remember to keep quiet when you are around your guinea pigs, as they are frightened by loud noises.

Try to find a time each day when you hand-feed your guinea pigs, and you will soon be a very welcome visitor!

Introductions

Guinea pigs are friendly animals so there should be no trouble if you introduce a newcomer to a hutch that already has guinea pigs. Put out plenty of food and arrange for the new guinea pig to arrive early in the day so that the guinea pigs have time to get to know each other before they go into their sleeping compartment.

Cavy Care

If you have other pets, such as cats or dogs, make sure they are always supervised when they are near your guinea pig's home.

Healthy Eating

Guinea pigs are not fussy feeders, but it is important to provide a suitable diet.

A guinea pig must have the correct balance of nutrients in its diet to grow, to stay healthy and to fight disease.

Every guinea pig needs:

• Hay
• Water
• Cereals and dried mix
• Green and root vegetables.

Hay

The wild ancestors of guinea pigs spent all day grazing on grass and plants, and pet guinea pigs are still grazing animals. In fact, they find it very hard to digest their food unless they have plenty of hay. Choose the softer meadow hay, and make sure it is always available in the hutch or cage.

Guinea pigs should be fed once a day.

Fruit and vegetables are an important part of the diet – and you can also offer them as treats. You can also buy seed-coated fruit sticks that you can hang in the cage.

Water

Guinea pigs need a supply of fresh, clean water.

Guinea pig diet

You can buy a complete food mix that has been specially prepared for guinea pigs. It will contain different cereals, grass pellets, and other essential nutrients, including added Vitamin C. Most small animals make their own Vitamin C. But guinea pigs, like us, have to be given it. You can find Vitamin C in fresh fruit and vegetables, which should be given to your guinea pigs every day, if you are not feeding a complete mix.

Favourite fresh foods include cauliflower, brussel sprouts, and chicory. You can also use plants from the garden, such as dandelion, groundsel and chickweed.

Guinea pigs need to gnaw to keep their teeth in good order, so hard, root vegetables, such as carrots and swedes should also be given. Do not give your pet 'wet' fresh foods, such as lettuce and tomatoes, as this can cause dietary problems.

Cavy Care

If guinea pigs do not have enough fruit and vegetables, they get a condition called scurvy. This is very painful, and can be fatal. It is prevented by feeding the right diet.

Guinea Pig Care

When you set up a home for your pet guinea pigs, you are responsible for all their needs.

If you are keeping two guinea pigs in a hutch or a cage, it will soon become dirty with droppings and with food remains.

Daily tasks
Find time every day to:

• Collect leftover food
• Refill the water bottle
• Clean the feeding bowls
• Spot clean by removing wet bedding and droppings.

Weekly tasks
Once a week you will need to clean the cage thoroughly with disinfectant and give your guinea pigs a fresh bed. Put your guinea pigs in their playpen or outside run while you are doing this.

Keep a close check on your guinea pig to ensure it is in good health.

If you choose a longhaired guinea pig, you will need to groom its coat.

Grooming

Smooth-haired guinea pigs do not need grooming. However, long-haired guinea pigs will need some help to keep the coat free from mats and tangles.

If you have chosen a long-haired or rough-haired (Abyssinian) guinea pig, you will need to introduce a grooming routine from an early age so that your guinea pig learns to relax while you do this.

You can buy grooming equipment at Pets At Home. Alternatively, a baby's toothbrush is ideal for grooming a guinea pig's coat.

Teeth

If you see your guinea pig drooling or struggling to eat, it may need its teeth clipped. This is a job for the vet.

Nails

If you keep your guinea pig on soft bedding, the nails do not wear down and will need to be clipped. Ask your vet, or an experienced guinea pig keeper, to do this for you.

Cavy Care

Remember that the outside run and playpen will also need to be kept clean and tidy.

Cavy Behaviour

Watch your guinea pigs closely and you will find out how they show their feelings.

Lying stretched out
This shows that the guinea pig is feeling relaxed and contented.

Stiff-legged trotting
You are most likely to see two males moving like this, as one tries to become the boss.

Mating dance
This is performed by a male guinea pig in front of a female that is ready for breeding. The dance consists of a series of hops, as the male wriggles his rear end. He may even spray urine at the sow.

Jumping
When a guinea pig is in high spirits it will suddenly jump from a standstill. This is known as 'pop-corning'.

Touching noses
Friendly guinea pigs will greet each other by touching noses.

Freezing
A guinea pig will freeze on the spot if it hears a strange sound or sees something that looks scary.

Guinea pig chatter
Guinea pigs use coos, chortles, squeaks and chirps when they are 'talking' to each other. If

Playing Dead
If a guinea pig sees an enemy and is very frightened, it will lie on its back, completely still. The guinea pig is pretending to be dead so the enemy will go away.

Guinea pigs are very sensitive to sound and will freeze if they hear anything unusual.

you have a close relationship with a guinea pig, it will even talk to you.

Cooing
This sound shows your guinea pig is content. A mother guinea pig coos to her babies, and sometimes a guinea pig will coo to its owner.

High-pitched squeak
This sound is made when a guinea pig has been hurt, or is very upset. Sometimes young guinea pigs squeak like this when they are missing their mother.

Chattering teeth
An angry guinea pig will

chatter its teeth to tell other guinea pigs to "stay away". If a guinea pig is roughly treated it may make this sound to its human handler.

Chortle
This throaty chuckle shows that a guinea pig is relaxed and happy. You may hear this sound when you are stroking your guinea pig.

Wheeeek!
This is made by guinea pigs when they see that food is on its way. Some guinea pigs will make this sound when they hear a bag rustle, or even when the refrigerator door is opened!

Index

Further Reading

C Collins Care for your
Guinea Pig

RSPCA
PET GUIDE

Available from
Pets At Home
Price £4.99

C Collins · family pet guides

GUINEA PIG

A practical
guide to
caring for
your guinea pig

Peter
Gurney

Available from
Pets At Home
Price £7.99